Watch Your Mouth

Choosing Words Which Honor Christ

Tom Lemler

Watch Your Mouth:
Choosing Words Which Honor Christ

ISBN-13: 978-0-9916326-8-8
ISBN-10: 0-9916326-8-0

For information:

Tom Lemler
Impact Prayer Ministry
2730 S Ironwood Dr
South Bend IN 46614
www.impactprayerministry.com
tlemler@gapministry.com

Every day you and I give people an impression of who Jesus is by the words we use. Are they hearing words which would draw them to Christ or push them away? Are you using words which draw you into greater relationship with God or words which create distance? I pray that this book will help you discover some of what God has to say about choosing words which honor Him.

This book is dedicated in grateful acknowledgment to God who has called me to use words wisely. I am thankful that He entrusts me with the task of sharing His Word as I have opportunity to preach and teach. I thank my dad, Irvin Lemler, who uses few words but has used them well in my life. I continue to thank my wife and daughter for their encouragement and support as I write. And I thank my good friend, Paul Stearns, for being such an encourager and fan of my writings. To all of these, and to you my readers, thank you!

Table of Contents

In Christ . . .

Introduction

He said what!? It's no big deal, it's just words! Far too often we put our brain in neutral and our mouth in overdrive; unleashing the "restless evil" that James calls the tongue. Jesus states that it is out of the overflow of the heart that the mouth speaks. As a follower of Jesus, our mouth ought to speak words that honor Him. Through time in prayer, this book was written to help you discover some of what the Bible says about ways to honor Christ with our words.

You may use this book as a thirty-one day devotional or go through it at whatever pace suits you. Take your time to let each statement about choosing your words sink deeply into your being. The book is designed to be used as both a devotional and a journal as you discover what God says about you.

Each topic follows the same three-page format. The first page is simply a statement of that day's focus and a scripture reference to get you started in God's Word. Look up the scripture reference and meditate on God's Word about the words He would have you speak.

The second page is some devotional writing that has come from my prayer time focused on that day's subject. It will include questions to help you think more clearly about the words you choose to use. There will be direction and suggestions on how to focus your prayer time as you seek to grow in relationship with God. As you go through this page of each day's topic, spend time with God in prayer for yourself and for the people around you to have a greater grasp of speaking God's way in Christ.

The third page is your turn to make this devotional even more personal! It contains a heading of the day's topic and then a blank lined page. This is for you to record your interaction with God each day. Jot down your thoughts, your prayers, other scriptures that God brings to mind during your time with Him, and/or changes in your attitude or actions (and words) that He reveals you need to make. Use this journal page to help you remember and to help you grow.

In prayer,
Tom Lemler
Impact Prayer Ministry

Day One

Choose Assuring Words

(Esther 9:30)

Choose Assuring Words

What things tend to make you anxious and fearful? Have you ever had someone try to assure you that things would be okay at a time when you had lost all hope? What does it take to help you have a more positive view of circumstances which look bleak? Are there specific words or phrases that help assure you when you are doubtful about a situation? How is God's Word useful in giving you assurance? How can you use God's Word to assure others? How often would your friends say you use words which bring assurance to them in times of their fears?

As the Jewish nation celebrated God's rescue of them through the courage of Esther, the queen and Mordecai wrote assuring words to all the people. These words were an assurance that this occasion would be remembered throughout time as a reminder of God's ability to rescue. As you pray, ask God to help you know the assurance He gives regarding His ability to rescue you. Pray that you would use words which assure others of God's desire and ability to be with them in the times of their greatest need.

Choose Assuring Words

Day Two

Choose Encouraging Words

(Acts 20:1-2)

Choose Encouraging Words

Who is your greatest encourager? What things do they do and say that you find encouraging? What part does tone and attitude have in the words you hear being encouraging? What words are most effective in helping you to overcome discouragement? How often do you find yourself speaking those words to others? Do you make it a practice to spread encouragement to others wherever you go?

Often times it is in the midst of great confusion and turmoil that a voice of encouragement is most needed. Following a riot in Ephesus, Paul spent time encouraging the believers in the city before continuing his travels. Even as he traveled, he stayed focused on speaking words of encouragement to the people he met. As you pray, ask God to help you gain words of encouragement through your time in His Word. Pray that the encouragement you receive from Him, and others, would be shared by you to all you meet. Pray for the wisdom to use encouraging words that fit each situation you face.

Choose Encouraging Words

Day Three

Choose Exhorting Words

(Hebrews 13:22)

Choose Exhorting Words

What comes to mind when you think of the word, exhortation? Is it a positive thought, negative thought, or somewhat neutral? When have you been most in need of being exhorted — urged or spurred on to action? Are there ways of delivering exhortation that makes it more likely to be heeded? How does your receptiveness to exhortation influence your ability to effectively exhort others? Are there things that make it easier for you to choose exhorting words when the people around you need to hear them?

The writer of Hebrews concludes the book with a request that the reader would bear with his words exhortation. Urging someone to follow through with right behavior is not always an easy thing to do and often not something that people eagerly listen to. As you pray, ask God to help you receive words of exhortation with an open heart, spirit, and mind. Pray that you would be filled with God's love when you need to choose exhorting words to speak to others. Pray for wisdom in exhorting others to love and good deeds.

Choose Exhorting Words

Day Four

Choose Gentle Words

(Proverbs 15:1 & 25:15)

Choose Gentle Words

When was the last time someone's harsh words have caused you pain? When do you think the last time was that your harsh words hurt someone? Is it easy to respond to the harshness of others with gentle words? What is required to do so? How have you been influenced by the gentle words of others? Have you experienced a dissolving of hurt and anger in your life through the gentle words that others have spoken to you?

The writer of Proverbs states that a gentle answer can turn away wrath but it can also break a bone! Gentle words are not a sign of weakness; rather they are a sign of appropriateness. We must choose gentle words because they are right. It is God's gentleness with us that restores us to Him. As you pray, ask God to give you a moldable heart that is filled with gentleness. Pray that the words you choose to use would reflect the gentleness that God has used with you. Pray that the people around you would see the Spirit of God in you as you speak gently to them. Pray that you would know how to combine truth and gentleness in your words.

Choose Gentle Words

Day Five

Choose Glorifying Words

(Romans 15:5-6)

Choose Glorifying Words

What first comes to mind when you hear the word glory? Have you ever talked, or heard someone talk, about returning something to its "glory days"? What is meant by that? What causes something, or someone, to no longer receive glory? How might unity among believers lead to words which glorify God? How does disunity hinder such glory? Do you give much thought to whether your everyday words glorify God? How could you glorify God with the words you use in everyday conversations?

A few years ago, a local sports team used the phrase "return to glory" as a rallying cry for their season. While a lot of this had to do with a desire for improved play, there was also an element of needing to change the way the program was being talked about. Sometimes our attitude removes glory from God when we fail to choose words which honor Christ. As you pray, ask God to help you give glory to Him through the words you use with the people around you. Pray that the unity you have with fellow believers would cause you to choose words which glorify God.

Choose Glorifying Words

Day Six

Choose Guarded Words

(Psalm 141:3)

Choose Guarded Words

How do you choose what to say? Do you believe that everything you think ought to be spoken? What do you think God's command to take every thought captive would say about that? Have you ever used words that you later wished you could take back? Could you? Does honesty require you to speak everything that comes to your mind? Have you ever been dishonest simply because you felt you had to say something? How can choosing guarded words help you to be honest with others?

We all know people who seem to blurt out some of the most inappropriate things at the most inopportune times -- perhaps we've been that person. As David prays, he asks God to set a guard over his mouth so it doesn't draw him into evil. Unguarded words have a way of causing pain and hurt to others and even to ourselves. As you pray, join the Psalmist in praying that God would set a guard over your mouth. Pray that you would engage your heart and mind before you put your tongue into overdrive. Pray that truth and love would guard the words you choose each day.

Choose Guarded Words

Day Seven

Choose Joyful Words

(Psalm 16:8-9)

Choose Joyful Words

Has your day ever been brightened by a note, text, or call from someone? Have you ever had the experience of a timely word bringing joy to your life? How do you feel when you can visibly see your words bring joy to another person? How does knowing God's presence is with you influence your expressions of joy? Does your faith give you reason to rejoice in all circumstances? How does expressing your joy in Christ help you overcome or endure difficult situations?

Often times when circumstances are difficult it is hard to remember God's command to express joy. You might want to look at what Paul means when he writes, "Rejoice always!", if you're trying to figure out when God commanded that. I'm the first to admit there are times when choosing joyful words is extremely difficult. As you pray, ask God to help you be constantly aware of His presence and the joy He brings into your life. Pray that you would learn how to be honest about your situations and still choose joyful words. Pray that the people around you would be encouraged by your words of joy.

Choose Joyful Words

Day Eight

Choose Just Words

(Psalm 37:30-31)

Choose Just Words

How important is it to you that your words are right and true? Do you value that at least as much as your desire for the words of others to be just? How do you define justice? Do you think your definition influences how you perceive words that are just? How do the laws of God help you understand true justice? How often do you think about using God's Word as the standard for the words you choose? How does your choice of words reflect the righteousness and wisdom which come from God?

Sometimes it is easier to choose words that you believe people want to hear rather than speak words that you know are right and true. It is our relationship with Christ that helps us to speak words that are needed in ways that are right. As you pray, ask God to help you understand His words to you which are just. Pray that God would give you the wisdom necessary to speak words that are just. Pray that the people around you would know because of the words you use that there is a way that is right and true. Pray that your words that are just would always be spoken in love.

Choose Just Words

Day Nine

Choose Known Words

(Psalm 139:4)

Choose Known Words

Which is easier for you, having a conversation with someone who has no idea what you are talking about or with someone who can finish your sentences? Have you ever tried talking with someone who seems to know the same words that you do but uses them in a completely different way? Are there times when you struggle for just the right word to say in a particular situation?

Some time back I received a call from a salesperson and when the call was finished my wife asked me what it was about. My honest answer was that I had no idea! The person was using words that I knew but in a way that had no meaning to me. Sometimes I think that happens when we pray. We try so hard to make our prayers sound like we think prayers ought to sound that we end up having no idea what we're talking about and completely miss what God wants to say to us. As you pray, take comfort in knowing that God knows the words of your heart even before they enter your mouth. Pray that you would have consistent time in God's Word so that you will know what His words will sound like.

Choose Known Words

Day Ten

Choose Living Words

(Acts 7:38)

Choose Living Words

Are there words that make you feel more alive when you hear them? Do you think the words you use often make others feel more alive? When you think of Moses receiving words from God, what first comes to mind? Do you often think about the laws of God being given as words which bring life? How does God's commentary that the words given to Moses on Mount Sinai were meant to be living words passed on to us change your view of them?

I've worked in a variety of places where I have allowed the discouraging words of my bosses to bring a sense of death to my mind. Their words definitely brought death to those specific jobs. I've also had coworkers and friends who have spoken encouraging words to me in the same situations. Sometimes the major difference between deadly words and living words is the attitude behind them and the attitude with which they are received. As you pray, ask God to help you accept His laws as living words in your life. Pray that you would be filled with His love as you speak to others about the Word of God -- the only words which can bring life eternal.

Choose Living Words

Day Eleven

Choose Overflowing Words

(Luke 6:45)

Choose Overflowing Words

What is your heart, mind, and soul filled with? How do you know? What types of words tend to flow the easiest from your mouth? Would your friends and family say you often use harsh words? Critical words? Angry words? Peaceful words? Loving words? Thoughtful words? Are you more likely to use words described in the chapters of this book or words that are opposite in nature? What would it take to change the words you use? How much effort will you put into doing so?

When something overflows, the thing that comes spilling out the top is representative of whatever is inside. The same is true of the things that overflow from our heart and spill out through our mouth. When I find that the words which flow from my mouth effortlessly are hurtful, angry words, then I know I need a heart check-up. As you pray, ask God to help you hear what kind of words overflow out of your heart and through your mouth. Pray that He would fill your heart with such good things that it is only good and beneficial words which overflow from your life. Pray that the people around you would be blessed by your godly words.

Choose Overflowing Words

Day Twelve

Choose Pleasant Words

(Proverbs 16:21, 24)

Choose Pleasant Words

When you think of the word pleasant, what first comes to mind? How much does what you hear influence the pleasantness of a particular place or situation? Have you ever been spoken to harshly? How did it make you feel in general? How did it make you feel toward the person speaking? How does a person's tone of voice affect your willingness to take instruction? Would the people around you say that the words you most often use are pleasant?

It is amazing how often people are willing to help if you ask nicely. I've been in a variety of situations when a pleasant word to a waitress or other service industry person brings about a remarkable change in their desire to serve. Few of us like to have things demanded of us, so why is the power of pleasant words such a surprise? As you pray, ask God to help you hear your speech, both in tone and content, from His perspective. Pray that you would stop and think about what pleasant words would sound like in every situation you face. Pray that you would represent Christ well by your choice of pleasant words.

Choose Pleasant Words

Day Thirteen

Choose Powerful Words

(1 Corinthians 2:4-5)

Choose Powerful Words

Have you ever been sold a product or idea by someone using slick, persuasive words? How do you feel when you realize that is what happened? How do you think that is different from someone using powerful words? What makes a word powerful? How often are you tempted to substitute gimmicks for real power? How does having a greater authority behind your words affect the power that they carry? How can you know that the words you use are powerful?

One of the greatest joys of ministry is seeing the power of God's Word transform a life. If you want to use powerful words instead of settling for words that are wise and persuasive by the world's standards, you must become familiar with God's Word. As you pray, ask God to help you grow in your determination not to settle. Pray that you would consume God's Word in a way that it is natural for you to use it in your daily speech. Pray that you would be bold enough to speak the most powerful word in the world -- the name of Jesus! Pray that the people around you would come to know Jesus through the words you choose.

Choose Powerful Words

Day Fourteen

Choose Praise-Filled Words

(Psalm 35:28)

Choose Praise-Filled Words

How often do you like to hear people say good things about you? Based on the words they hear from you, what would people think about your feelings toward God? Are you more likely to talk about your struggles with disappointments in life or about how God has carried you through them? Do you think your attitude toward life, and God, would change if you consistently chose praise-filled words? How should God's rescue of you from sin affect your desire to praise Him?

On-line reviews can be a complicated maze to work through when trying to determine a good place to visit or product to buy. It seems everything has its share of fans as well as those who are disgruntled. Sometimes I think people view a relationship with God that way too. They have interest but they carefully evaluate what those who already know God say by their words and actions. As you pray, ask God to fill your mouth with praise at all times. Pray that you would learn to praise Him in times you consider good and in times you consider bad. Pray that the people around you would hear a good review of God through the praise that is on your lips.

Choose Praise-Filled Words

Day Fifteen

Choose Prayerful Words

(1 Kings 8:59-60)

(Psalm 54:2)

Choose Prayerful Words

How would you describe your prayer life? Are you an act first, pray later person? A pray first and act accordingly person? Or is prayer something that seems impossible for you to figure out? What is your first thought or reaction when you hear the verse, "Pray without ceasing."? Do you think your life would be different if you gave thought to choosing prayerful words in all circumstances? How have the prayerful words of someone else been an influence in your life?

As one who has an unhealthy fear of people, God has always been the one I could talk with about anything. But even having that comfort level when it comes to prayer, I must admit that I don't use prayerful words with others as often as I should. To use prayerful words more often, we must be deliberate in our listening to God and hearing what people are actually saying. As you pray, thank God for always listening when you go to Him. Pray that He would help you remember to seek Him for prayerful words to use in your conversations with others. Pray that the people around you would value the wisdom that comes from prayerful words.

Choose Prayerful Words

Day Sixteen

Choose Promised Words

(Psalm 66:13-14)

Choose Promised Words

How important is it to you that you keep your promises? How do you feel when people make promises to you that they do not keep? How faithful has God been to you in keeping His promises that are found in His Word? What kind of promises do you make to God? How consistent are you in keeping them? Do you view your immersion into Christ as a promise you made to Him? As a promise He made to you?

When in trouble, people are often quick to promise anything that they think will rescue them from the troublesome circumstance. When out of trouble, the remembrance of the former promise is sometimes rather vague. When we become a Christian, we promise God that we belong to Him forever and He promises to be our God completely. As you pray, ask God to help you recall any promises you have made that you have not yet kept. Pray that you would speak words of promise that are backed by a firm commitment of doing. Pray that you would represent God's faithfulness by the way you share His promises with others.

Choose Promised Words

Day Seventeen

Choose Pure Words

(Psalm 17:3)

Choose Pure Words

How important is purity to you? Does that answer change depending on what we attach the word pure to? Are you concerned about the purity of the food and water you eat and drink? Why? Have you ever thought about the purity of the words you use, and listen to, being even more important than the purity of your food and drink? How do you feel when you know pure words are being spoken to you? How will you use pure words to protect your heart and encourage others?

In today's culture, sexual purity is probably the first thing that comes to mind when most people hear the word purity. While that is an important area of purity, God teaches that impurity in any area of our life comes as a result of our thoughts and words. James says that if anyone could completely control their tongue they would be a perfect person. As you pray, ask God to help you listen to the pure words that are found in scripture. Pray that the words that come from your mouth would always be pure in content and intent as you seek to build up others according to their need.

Choose Pure Words

Day Eighteen

Choose Reliable Words

(Proverbs 22:20-21)

Choose Reliable Words

Do you know anyone with a reputation of "being as good as their word"? What do you think of when you hear that phrase? Would the people around you say that you are a person of your word? What things make the words of some people seem to be more reliable than those of others? Do you believe the Bible to be the reliable words of God? How often do you turn to the Word of God to choose reliable words? How does choosing reliable words help you to give sound answers to those you are accountable to?

When we hear, or use, words that appear to have no intention of being kept, trust is often an early casualty. Our commitment to choosing reliable words helps other to not only trust us, but to trust the things we say about our relationship with God. As you pray, ask God to help you weigh your words carefully in considering how reliable they are. Pray that you would know the reliability of the words of others before you even consider sharing them. Pray that your word choices would help you to be a reliable witness to others of the power of Christ in you.

Choose Reliable Words

Day Nineteen

Choose Restrained Words

(Proverbs 17:27)

Choose Restrained Words

How often do you find yourself "biting your tongue"? Do you view that practice as a good thing or bad? Why? How does being filled with godly knowledge help a person have restraint with their words? Have you ever been injured by words spoken rashly? Have your unrestrained words ever injured someone? What did you do about it? What should you? Why does it seem so difficult for most people to choose restrained words?

Here in the United States, we pride ourselves on having a freedom of speech that can't be taken away from us. Because we often hear about our first amendment rights, we start to believe we must exercise that right at every opportunity. Many act as if when a thought enters their mind, they must express it as soon as possible. God calls for us to choose restrained words so that we consider His perspective before we speak. As you pray, ask God to help you to put a reign on your tongue. Pray that you would always take the time to hear how something might sound before you actually speak it. Pray that God would fill you with the wisdom to know when to speak words which have been restrained.

Choose Restrained Words

Day Twenty

Choose Satisfying Words

(Proverbs 18:20)

Choose Satisfying Words

What has been the most satisfying meal you have ever eaten? What made it so? How would those reasons apply to words that are satisfying? What is the most satisfying thing someone has said to you? What made it so? Have you ever had words which left “a sour taste in your mouth”? What about them was so unpleasant? Do you think the people around you would say the words you use are satisfying to you? To the hearer?

Most people want to find satisfaction not only in the things they do, but also in the things they hear and say. Many times when we are frustrated by the words we hear coming toward us, it is because we have ignored God’s principle that we will reap what we sow. Choosing satisfying words will not only benefit those who hear them, but they are seeds that will return a harvest of satisfaction in our own life. As you pray, ask God to help you consider the words you use. Pray that you would use the words spoken to you as a tool in examining how satisfying the words you speak to others might be. Pray that you would chose the Words of Life which satisfy completely.

Choose Satisfying Words

Day Twenty - One

Choose Solemn Words

(Deuteronomy 32:46)

Choose Solemn Words

What types of events do you think of as being solemn occasions? As you think about what makes them so, how would those traits carry over into the idea of solemn words? Have you ever had someone tell you something that you took completely serious only to have them add later, "Just kidding!"? How did you feel? Do people know you as one who can be serious when you need to be or do they tend to laugh you off when you try to be serious? Why?

If you have ever had someone not follow through with something you had asked only to be told they didn't think you were serious, you can probably understand the reason God describes the final instruction from Moses to the Israelites as being "solemnly declared". There are things we often joke about and probably shouldn't take too seriously, but there are also things of great importance that require us to use solemn words. As you pray, ask God to help you speak in ways that people will take the important things you say seriously. Pray that you would be filled with loving words that also express the seriousness of having a relationship with Jesus.

Choose Solemn Words

Day Twenty-Two

Choose Spirit-Filled Words

(2 Samuel 23:2)

Choose Spirit-Filled Words

Are there people that you listen to who seem to have words that are filled with wisdom beyond their training? How often do you think about the presence of God's Spirit living in you? In your religious practice, how open are people to consider the working of God's Spirit in an individual's life? What would Spirit-filled words sound like? How would you recognize them? Where did what we have as the written Word of God come from? What might that say about a starting point for choosing Spirit-filled words?

One of my mentors use to say in teaching about listening to God, "If God did all of the work to put His Spirit within you, don't you think His Spirit might have a few things to say to you?". God says that all scripture is God-breathed and written by men, not of their own will but carried along by the Spirit. As you pray, ask God to help you use His Word as a starting point for Spirit-filled words in your life. Pray that you would grow in your recognition of, and listening to, His Spirit God has put within you. Pray that the words you choose would always be Spirit-filled words.

Choose Spirit-Filled Words

Day Twenty-Three

Choose Strengthening Words

(1 Thessalonians 4:18)

(2 Thessalonians 2:16-17)

Choose Strengthening Words

How have the words of others helped you to overcome, or persevere, in times when you were weak? What about their words gave you strength? Do you think the people around you would say they are strengthened or weakened by your words? Or some of both? How does God's grace in your life add strength to your words? Do you find grace-filled words to be more strengthening than legalistic words? Which do you find yourself using more than the other?

There are days when I seem to hit bottom and a weakness in my mind seems to trigger a switch, turning on an anxiety-fueled panic attack. In the midst of these attacks, I turn to God's Word and songs about God's character to strengthen me in my weakness. Each time, these words are about God's grace, love, mercy, compassion, patience, understanding, and a variety of other things that communicate He understands and I'm still His. As you pray, ask God to strengthen you by His Word. Pray that the words you speak to others would strengthen them when they are weak.

Choose Strengthening Words

Day Twenty-Four

Choose Teaching Words

(Psalm 78:1)

Choose Teaching Words

Who do you take instruction from? How do you decide if something is good instruction? Who is the teacher that has made the longest-lasting impression in your life? Why? What are some things that you have taught, or could teach, others? How does it make you feel to know that there are currently people learning something from you simply by observing the way you live? Does knowing that make you want to be more deliberate in choosing teaching words?

People often say that life is a test. While I understand what they mean, I think life is really more like a series of instructional times with the primary test being the final exam at the end of life. The responsibility of every Christian is to not only learn the lessons in life needed to be prepared for the final exam, but to teach in every way possible how others can be ready for an eternity with God. As you pray, ask God to help you choose teaching words that will instruct others in the way they ought to walk. Pray that you would make the most of every opportunity to help someone grow in their relationship with Christ through your teaching.

Choose Teaching Words

Day Twenty-Five

Choose Tested Words

(Genesis 42:16)

Choose Tested Words

What do you do when you hear something that you are not sure is true? Do you believe every promise that people make to you? What things make you more likely to believe what someone says? How do you feel when someone wants to test the accuracy of your words? Are there people in your life of whom you would trust anything they said because their words have always stood the test of time? What would it take for you to become one of those people?

Most of us have people we trust to do what they say and people we don't. A lot of factors may go into that, but one of the most common reasons for not believing what a person says is that their words have been tested in the past and found wanting. If you find that you are often not believed, you may want to spend time with God examining if you speak trusted words. As you pray, ask God to help you speak only words which can be trusted. Pray that the words you speak about God would not simply be theory and Bible stories, but would be tested words that you have discovered through your relationship with Jesus.

Choose Tested Words

Day Twenty-Six

Choose Timely Words

(Proverbs 15:23)

Choose Timely Words

No pointing fingers, but have you ever known someone that seems to always say the right thing (or maybe the wrong thing) at the worst moment possible? Have you ever been in a situation where you needed a word of encouragement or comfort that just never came? Have you ever felt you needed to say something to a person but wrestled with the "when" so long that nothing was ever said? When was the most memorable time that a person spoke a timely word into your life?

Some say that in communication, timing is everything and that just may be true. We've probably all suffered through the ill-timed words of others and have enjoyed the receiving end of well-timed words. And we've probably all been on the giving end of each of those as well. As you pray, ask God to help you speak timely words that are good into the lives of the people around you. Pray that you would allow His timely words to you give you the courage to listen for the promptings of His Spirit in knowing when to speak the right words to others.

Choose Timely Words

Day Twenty-Seven

Choose Truthful Words

(Psalm 119:43)

Choose Truthful Words

How do you feel when you discover someone has deliberately lied to you? Can a person be deceptive even when the words used are technically true? When you consider the truthfulness of something, what is the basis for your conclusion? What is the most necessary companion to truthful words? Where would you go to find examples of truthful words spoken in love? How confident are you that you are speaking truthful words when you share the Word of God?

Truth spoken with the wrong attitude and motives can do great damage yet the same truth spoken with compassion and in love can bring healing and restoration. It is important when you choose truthful words that you use them in line with the instructions God give us in His Word. As a Christian, your words ought to build up and encourage without shaming and tearing down the listener. As you pray, ask God to fill you with His love for people so that your truthful words would always be spoken with an attitude of concern for the listener. Pray that the truthful words you choose would have their foundation in God's Word.

Choose Truthful Words

Day Twenty-Eight

Choose Warning Words

(Acts 2:40)

Choose Warning Words

Have you ever ignored a warning that you later wished you had heeded? Have you ever been in a situation where someone could have warned you of potential trouble but chose not to and you wished that they would have? When you anticipate trouble, how do you decide when to warn someone? Does the refusal of people to heed your warnings influence your decision to choose warning words? Does your response to warning words change the willingness of others to warn you in the future?

Throughout scripture, God warns that there are consequences for our actions yet many live as if this isn't true. Sometimes we fail to heed warnings because we don't think they apply to us or we don't want to submit to the person issuing the warning. As you pray, ask God to help you understand that the warnings He gives are for your good and for the good of mankind. Pray that you would have the courage to warn others of the consequences, according to God's word, of a life apart from Jesus.

Choose Warning Words

Day Twenty-Nine

Choose Well-Spoken Words

(Psalm 141:5-6)

Choose Well-Spoken Words

What would make a word be well-spoken? Have you ever been in a situation when words from the past come to mind and you realize because of their value now, just how well-spoken they were? How do you feel when someone says something that doesn't seem to fit with the current conversation? Are you more likely to recognize a well-spoken word when it is spoken or when it is needed? What is the value of a well-spoken word if no one seems to heed it at the time it is said?

My mind has a wiring pattern that requires great contemplation before determining the value of things that are said. Rarely do I hear something and immediately think, "That was some well-spoken advice." The true value of well-spoken words isn't in how quickly they are accepted, rather in the long-lasting truth they contain. As you pray, ask God to give you the courage to choose well-spoken words even when they don't seem to be heeded immediately. Pray that God's Spirit would continue to work in the minds of the people listening so that at just the right time, they would see the value of your words.

Choose Well-Spoken Words

Day Thirty

Choose Wise Words

(Psalm 37:30, 49:3)

Choose Wise Words

What is the wisest advice you have ever been given? Who shared it with you? What was their source? For you, what makes certain words seem foolish? Do you ever struggle to have just the right words to share with someone? Where do you turn when you need help choosing wise words to use? Does choosing wise words mean that everyone will finally pay attention to what you are saying? Why not?

In the book of James, we read that if anyone lacks wisdom they should ask of God who gives generously and without finding fault. At times it is amazing just how much foolish talk exists when God has promised a never-failing resource to help us choose wise words. If you want to speak words of wisdom on a more consistent basis, spend time with God and His Word on a more consistent basis. As you pray, ask God to not only give you the wisdom He has promised, but to give you the courage to share the wisdom He has put within you. Pray that He would fill you with a humility that allows you to share wise words in a manner that makes people want to hear them.

Choose Wise Words

Day Thirty - One

Choose Worthy Words

(Jeremiah 15:19)

Choose Worthy Words

What are words worth to you? Do different words have different value? Does the person speaking them change the value of any given words? Does the way in which you say the exact same words change their value? Why? Who determines the worth of words and decides the value they have or don't have? Which would your friends say comes more naturally from you, speaking worthy words or unworthy words? Why?

When I first added this topic to the book, my mind kept thinking of how important it is to use words that are worth something. As a preacher, teacher, and writer, words are one of the major tools of my trade. Normally I weigh my words very carefully and consider their worth in the setting I plan to use them. Most importantly, I spend time in prayer asking God to edit my words so that the ones I end up using are the ones that have worth in His view. As you pray, ask God to help you seek Him as the ultimate source for words that are worthy. Pray that you would also see Him as the primary audience for the worthy words you use.

Choose Worthy Words

Bonus Day

Choose God's Words

(Numbers 23:12)

Choose God's Words

How often do you pause before you speak? Do you give much thought to choosing words that God would want you to speak? Do you ever find yourself saying words because you believe they are the words your listener wants to hear? How much does peer pressure influence the words you choose? What would be some hindrances to always choosing God's words? Are there times or situations when you really don't want to choose God's words? Why?

I tend to pause a lot before I speak and even while I'm speaking. In doing so, I find that people who don't know me often assume I have nothing to say or that I'm finished, so they rush in with a multitude of words which spill from their mouth. The initial reason for my speech pattern is simply about the way my mind is wired but I've discovered that it is a good pattern to cultivate if I really want to choose God's words. As you pray, ask God to help you grow in your desire to speak only words that honor Him and have Him as their source. Pray that you would be familiar enough with scripture that you would recognize God's words in everyday life.

Choose God's Words